BACH FOR CLARINET

Bach

THAT'S EASY! ™

Wise Publications
London/New York/Paris/Sydney/Copenhagen/Madrid

Exclusive Distributors:
Music Sales Limited
8/9 Frith Street, London W1V 5TZ, England.
Music Sales Pty Limited
120 Rothschild Avenue,
Rosebery, NSW 2018, Australia.

This book © Copyright 1994 by
Wise Publications
Order No. AM91871
ISBN 0-7119-3983-7

Music processed by Interactive Sciences Limited, Gloucester
Designed by Hutton & Partners

Music Sales' complete catalogue describes thousands of titles and is available in full colour sections by subject, direct from
Music Sales Limited. Please state your areas of interest and send a cheque/postal order for £1.50 for postage to:
Music Sales Limited, Newmarket Road, Bury St. Edmunds, Suffolk IP33 3YB.

Your Guarantee of Quality
As publishers, we strive to produce every book to the highest commercial standards.

The music has been freshly engraved and the book has been carefully designed to minimise
awkward page turns and to make playing from it a real pleasure.

Particular care has been given to specifying acid-free, neutral-sized paper made from pulps which have not been
elemental chlorine bleached. This pulp is from farmed sustainable forests and was produced with special regard for the
environment. Throughout, the printing and binding have been planned to ensure a sturdy, attractive publication
which should give years of enjoyment.

If your copy fails to meet our high standards, please inform us and we will gladly replace it.

Printed in the United Kingdom by
Caligraving Limited, Thetford, Norfolk.

CONTENTS

Air
from Suite in F

Moderately

Air
from The Peasant Cantata

Moderately

Air in D Major
from Orchestral Suite in D

Aria

Moderately

Badinerie
from Orchestral Suite in B minor

Bourrée

Bourrée No. 1
from French Overture

Moderately

Bourrée No. 1
from Orchestral Suite in C

Come Sweetest Death, Come, Blessed Rest

Slow

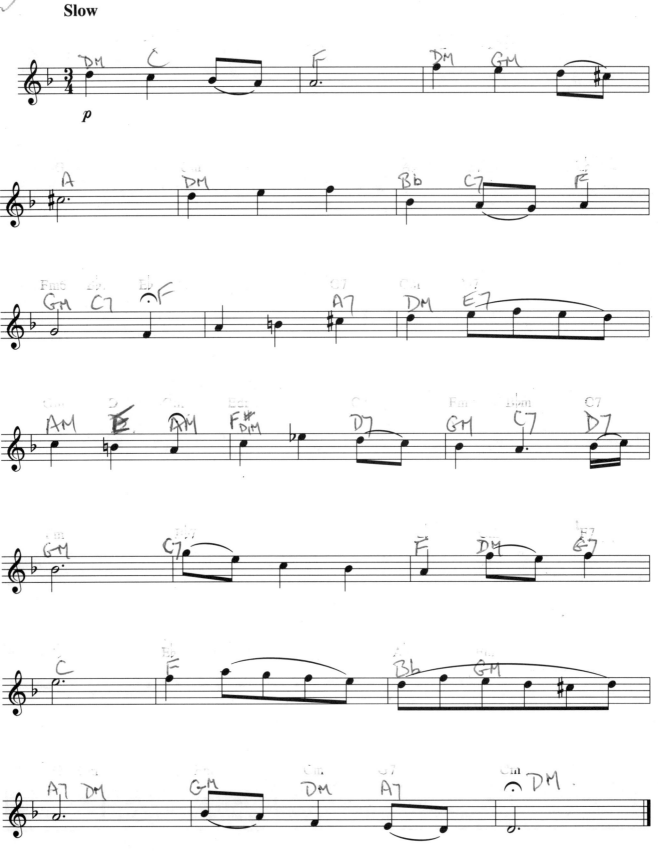

In Tears Of Grief
from St Matthew Passion

Moderately

Jesu, Joy Of Man's Desiring

With easy movement

Lie Still, O Sacred Limbs
from St John Passion

Moderately

March

With movement

Minuet
from Orchestral Suite No. 2 in B Minor

Moderately

Minuet in C Minor

Moderately

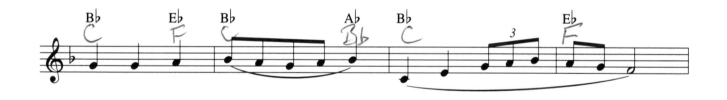

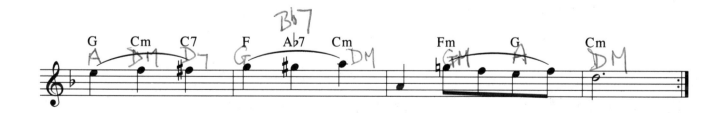

Minuet in D Minor

Moderately

Minuet in G

Moderately

Minuet in G Minor

Moderately

Musette

Moderately

Passepied No. 1
from Orchestral Suite in C

Bright

Prelude in E Minor
from Eight Short Preludes & Fugues for Organ

Prepare Thyself, Zion
from Christmas Oratorio

Rinkart
from Kommt Seelen

Sarabande
from Cello Suite in E♭

Moderately

Sarabande
from Sonata Nach Reincken

Moderately

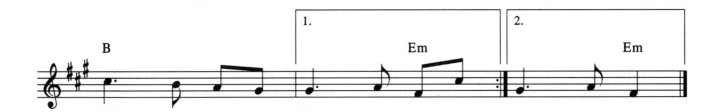

Sarabande
from Suite in E♭

Moderately

Sheep May Safely Graze

Moderately

Sleepers, Wake! A Voice Is Calling

Moderately

rall.